To
social workers
in training

Mummy

Little People, **BIG DREAMS**

ROSA PARKS

Little People, BIG DREAMS
ROSA PARKS

Written by
Lisbeth Kaiser

Illustrated by
Marta Antelo

Frances Lincoln
Children's Books

Rosa grew up near Montgomery, Alabama, with her mother, brother, and grandparents.

She was very little and very brave, and she always tried to do what was right.

When she was young, Rosa's grandparents told her stories about slavery, when black people weren't free to live like other people.

Slavery was over, but times were still hard for Rosa and her family. Black people were treated very badly and told they were not equal to white people.

Every day, Rosa watched the school bus go by taking white children to their big school. It didn't stop for her. She had to walk a long way to the one-room school that was just for black children.

Rosa knew this wasn't right. She knew she was a regular person, just as good as anyone else.

Lots of times, she had to make sure other people knew it too.

When Rosa grew up and got a job in the city, she couldn't use the same doors, elevators, bathrooms, or water fountains as white people.

She could ride the bus, but she had to sit in the back. Her life was full of rules that she knew weren't right.

Rosa fell in love with a man named Raymond who was
trying to change the rules to be more fair and equal.

Soon Rosa started working, too, trying to get more rights for black people and help for those who were treated badly. She worked day after day, even when it seemed like nothing would ever change.

On her way home from the city one day, a bus driver told Rosa to stand up so a white person could take her seat. She was sick of rules that she knew were wrong. She thought, *enough*. She said, "No."

Rosa was taken to jail. She wasn't scared, because she knew that what she was fighting for was right.

When Rosa came home that night, she talked with her friends and family about what to do. She decided to keep fighting, no matter how hard it would be.

Black people all over the city heard what had happened to Rosa.
They thought, *enough.*

Rosa inspired them to stop riding the buses until the rules changed.

So they walked, to school and to work and to the store, in all kinds of weather.

Rosa traveled the country—from New York to San Francisco—to convince other people to join the fight.

Finally, after one year, the Supreme Court decided that treating black people differently from white people on buses was wrong. The rules were going to change!

It was no longer safe for Rosa to live in Alabama. She moved to Detroit and fought for fair schools, jobs, and houses for black people.

She fought for voting rights, women's rights,
and the rights of people in prison.

When Rosa was an older woman, she was given awards and told she was a hero. But she knew who she was.

A regular person, just as good as
anyone else. And she had work to do.

ROSA PARKS

(Born 1913 • Died 2005)

c. 1950

1955

Rosa Parks was an American activist and one of the most important figures in the civil rights movement. The grandchild of former slaves, she grew up with her mother, brother, and grandparents on a small farm outside of Montgomery, Alabama, where she faced mean and unfair treatment because of her skin color. She regularly resisted with bravery and dignity. It wasn't until she met her husband, Raymond Parks, that she learned about activism. At 30, she became a leader in the National Association for the Advancement of Colored People (NAACP) in Montgomery and began working to end inequality.

1965   1984

When she was 42, Rosa was taken from a bus and jailed because
she refused to give her seat to a white person. Her arrest brought
the black people of Montgomery together to demand change and
she helped lead them in a year-long boycott of the buses. Rosa's
actions and hard work helped establish the civil rights movement.
They also cost her family their jobs and safety. They moved north
to Detroit, where Rosa was dismayed to find that great inequality
persisted. She remained an activist for the rest of her life, helping
many people and inspiring countless others with her bravery, dignity,
and determination in the ongoing fight for human equality.

Want to find out more about **Rosa Parks**?

She has written a book about her life:

I am Rosa Parks by Rosa Parks and James Haskins

You could also try these:

I am Rosa Parks by Brad Meltzer

Who Was Rosa Parks? by Yona Zeldis McDonough

And if you're near the Henry Ford Museum in Michigan, you could even visit the famous Rosa Parks bus.

Quarto is the authority on a wide range of topics.

Quarto educates, entertains and enriches the lives of our readers—enthusiasts and lovers of hands-on living.

www.quartoknows.com

First published in the U.S.A. in 2017 by Frances Lincoln Children's Books,
an imprint of The Quarto Group,
142 W 36th Street, 4th Floor, New York, NY 10018, U.S.A. QuartoKnows.com
Visit our blogs at QuartoKids.com

Text copyright © 2017 by Lisbeth Kaiser
Illustrations copyright © 2017 by Marta Antelo

This book has not been authorized or endorsed by the Rosa Parks Estate. Any mistakes herein are the fault of the publishers, who would be happy to rectify them on a future printing.

Commissioned as part of the Little People, Big Dreams series,
conceived by Mª Isabel Sánchez Vegara.
Originally published under the title Pequeña & Grande by Alba Editorial (www.albaeditorial.es)

ISBN 978-1-78603-018-4

Printed in China

1 3 5 7 9 8 6 4 2

MIX
Paper from
responsible sources
FSC® C008047

Photographic acknowledgements (pages 28-29, from left to right) 1. Rosa Parks Collection at the Library of Congress, 2015 © The Washington Post, Getty Images 2. Rosa Louise McCauley Parks booking photo, 1955 © Universal Images Group, Getty Images 3. Selma to Montgomery March, 1965 © Stephen F. Somerstein, Getty Images 4. Rosa Parks Protesting Apartheid, 1984 © Bettman, Getty Images

Also in the *Little People,* **BIG DREAMS** series:

FRIDA KAHLO

ISBN: 978-1-84780-783-0

Meet Frida Kahlo, one of the best artists of the twentieth century.

COCO CHANEL

ISBN: 978-1-84780-784-7

Discover the life of Coco Chanel, the famous fashion designer.

MAYA ANGELOU

ISBN: 978-1-84780-889-9

Read about Maya Angelou—one of the world's most beloved writers.

AMELIA EARHART

ISBN: 978-1-84780-888-2

Learn about Amelia Earhart—the first female to fly solo over the Atlantic.

AGATHA CHRISTIE

ISBN: 978-1-84780-960-5

Meet the queen of the imaginative mystery—Agatha Christie.

MARIE CURIE

ISBN: 978-1-84780-962-9

Be introduced to Marie Curie, the Nobel Prize-winning scientist.

EMMELINE PANKHURST

ISBN: 978-1-78603-020-7

Meet Emmeline Pankhurst, the suffragette who helped women get the vote.

AUDREY HEPBURN

ISBN: 978-1-78603-053-5

Learn about the iconic actress and humanitarian—Audrey Hepburn.